A beginners guide to becoming a good manager!

A guide for anyone who wants to succeed at their first management job.

Jason Dearn

A beginners guide to becoming a good manager

Published by Lulu.inc

The Self-publishing website.

www.lulu.com

ISBN 978-1-4452-1922-6

Cover by Lulu, Inc.

www.pilotbank.co.uk

admin@pilotbank.co.uk

A beginners guide to becoming a good manager

Other books by Jason Dearn available on www.lulu.com

The absolute beginners guide to becoming a pilot.

A beginners guide to becoming a good manager

Contents

Introduction

Jason Dearn has spent 24 years in retail. Of those years, 20 of them have been in a variety of management roles. He has worked for five retail companies in over 130 different locations and has enjoyed working with thousands of different people.

The book is a guide for the new manager on how to become a good new manager, to give you an insight on some of the useful tools, lessons in plain English. Having been in so many new situations, and generally having learned the hard way, It is hopefully, a tool for the reader to avoid some of the dumbass mistakes he has made. Freedom to fail…lol.

Jason currently lives in the West Midlands of the United Kingdom, fly's helicopters, writes books and loves to eat pizza.

A beginners guide to becoming a good manager

For Louise – Thanks for being you!

Chapter One

So you got the Job

Well done! Now, this is where the metal meets the meat! You have been the interview, the second interview or the assessment centre and sailed through it. On the other hand, your boss had spotted your talent, and has promoted you onto a fast track Program and is expecting great things of you. Maybe you have started up on your own, got that great idea and set up your own company. All of these are examples of first time managers coming into the dark and shadowy world of people and project management.
This can be daunting, think of all of the things that come with the new role; Responsibility, people, legals, deadlines, the boss, the staff, projects, worry, life balance, budgets and many many more.

Being a manager for the first time is hard. From day one, the people you manage have expectations from you, your boss has expectations from you, your customer, both internal and external have expectations of you. The problems start to arise when your output or performance doesn't match up with each of the groups and you try, and invariably fail, to meet anyone's demands. The first day on the job can be an awful experience, as you arrive at the top of your game and by the end of the day, you will (hopefully) understand what is expected of you. If not you could be in trouble.

The smart manager will seek help, but more often than not, the failure to accept that you need help will stop you asking for it. This is foolish at best and at worst a career breaker. Being a manager, unless you are very lucky, is not a god given skill that is bestowed upon you whilst you read the offer letter, or while you sleep the up skilling fairy drops it of in the back of your head. You have to learn it, or in some cases earn it.

All interviews for first time managers are a wild stab in the dark for the employer. The key measure any interviewer relies upon is past performance, a new manager has no real past performance to be judged upon. So as the employer, or your direct line manager, there is usually a measure of expectation from previous new manager's performance, which you will be gauged upon. This seems a little unfair, but, there is very little else for them to base a judgement upon.

So you have basically been landed into a role which you have had no, or little experience of, and a set of measures which others have set as the standard. This really is a no win situation for the new manager who doesn't firstly realise he or she is out of their depth and secondly does nothing about it.

So, what can you do? Well buying or reading this book, you have taken a positive step. It will help you with some very basic skills that you can arm you for the challenges ahead and ensure that you have a fighting chance of succeeding in your chosen profession.

So what is a manager?

In a nutshell, the manager (at any level) has the responsibility to deliver a set objectives or targets, with a set amount of resources in a specific period.

Managers generally have a manager. This is often a misconception with new managers, the new manager can begin to consider that because they have been elevated into a new position, that they have less responsibility to actually be at the sharp end of any operation. They also tend to believe, that that every call they make is the right call. This generally is not the case. The managers manager will have higher expectations of the new manager, and if you start your new role believing that you can do no wrong then you will crash and burn.

I want you to consider yourself as the piggy in the middle. As already mentioned, your first role will catapult you into the middle of a minefield of expectations and considerations. Both your staff and you boss has both expectations and considerations, your job is to manage these four, often polar, points of view.

The book, how do we use it?

Simple. There are 10 chapters in the book. The ones from three to nine explain a skill in each. What that skill is, how to use it and the up shot of using it.

The final chapter is the trick shot chapter, using them all together or in combinations to get the best out of you and the job you have been given.

I have tried to keep the terminology simple, so it is easy to integrate into your working life. I have also listed other management books that you might be interested in reading to support you learning.

Chapter Two

A day in the life of the new manager

Like all managers, I was once a newly appointed manager. My first stint at managing was not my finest hour. I was completely unprepared for what was to come. I was 19 or maybe 20, and I started my career in management as a retailer, I was a newly appointed produce manager in the bottom store, of a very competitive group of stores. I had changed groups for my first appointment, having been the assistant manager on a dept in the current flagship store on my previous group. Prior to that, I completed a stint in the previous flagship store. I did not want to be appointed in to this job. This may sound strange now, but I had definitely not wanted it. I had a great place to work, and to say I was forced into the role was an understatement. I remember sitting in the office with my Stores area manager and telling him, I didn't want to go. In the end I was going, I only agreed on the proviso that, if it did not work out, I could go back. So I was appointed. I had ended up in a store that had no resources, not taking a lot of money, on a group where I knew no one, and had no one really to call on for support. My boss didn't want to know really, I wasn't his first choice, in fact I think I had been appointed whilst he was on holiday. It didn't start well, the staff were not trusting of me, the store populace all knew one another and I was an unknown outsider, the management team consisted of the worst performing store manager on the group who unknown to me at the time, was in there as a punishment for bullying. The deputy was a good bloke, and the Ast manager was straight out of the new manager program. It got worst still, the manager I was replacing was universally liked, and the general populace had expected his number two to be made up. Then I appeared.

I was doomed to fail. I had no experience in low volume store, I had no experience in dealing with the boss, I had not made a good impression with the staff and it was not going to get any better. I remember being in ear shot of one of the staff, who was so engrossed in his conversation that he didn't notice I was there and he was running me down and pointing out all of my faults as a human being, let alone as his manager. I began to get more and more de-motivated and despondent. I had been forced into a position that I had not been ready for, I couldn't see a way out of the problem, nothing I seemed to do was right, nothing I said or did had any affect. My first appointment had been the equivalent of a bad motorway shunt, just general carnage.

The upshot of this was that after 3 months I stepped down and went back to another store as a deputy department manager. It took me three years to get back on the promotion bus, in the mean time I had a chance to reflect upon the time I had had, and started reading books on becoming a manager. My first experience of management has directly affected the course of my life and given me the information and experience to write down these tricks and hints for you to arm yourself with on that first appointment. I genuinely hope that the following pages prevent you the new manager, from going through the experience that I went through in my early career. In addition, I want you to learn from my mistakes and prosper. A stigma of failure is very hard to remove, it was once said to me that you need to earn a reputation and not be given one!

I had to work very hard to get rid of the one I had been given, and earn the one I wanted!

So, lets get on with it!

Chapter Three

Managing you

The First lesson on being a successful new manager is to be able to manage yourself. Managing yourself is a key skill of all successful managers.

So, what do I mean by managing yourself? Well, how can you effectively manage a group of staff or a project without being organized? The simple answer is that you cannot.

One thing that all managers have in common, whether good or bad, is the fact that we are all human (sometimes you may think your boss isn't, however trust me they are!). As humans, we have commitments and lives outside of our work place, as managers, the job will start to impact upon this life. Most of the impacts need to managed or you will start to become de-motivated with the job itself.

Secondly, you now have responsibilities to the people relying on you, such as the staff and your colleagues, or the other departments, branches or customers. Without ensuring you have a plan, or that you are organised, you will quickly become bogged down, and spending long precious time trying to sort out problems and them affecting how you complete the job in hand.

In the previous chapter, we discussed the disastrous day in the life of a new, unarmed manager (mine!), as we saw the impacts of these blind fumblings in the dark. The new manager can very quickly become despondent with the job and their performance can start to dip!

So how should you manage yourself?

The key is to plan. In many, many companies you will be introduced to the concept of PLAN – DO – REVIEW. This is a basic, very well known theory.

The new manager can fall into the trap of being, "innocently over managed", again, this is down to the way that managers are taught to manage. The theory behind this over management is the Direction, Support, Coaching and Delegation model. Managers will use a method of job allocation, which is suitable for the persons (employee, or new manager) current skill level.

An example of this is, when the new manager is appointed into a new department, which they have no experience in, and their immediate line manager will DIRECT them in the jobs, or tasks that need to be completed. This can be very frustrating for the new manager, considering that they are highly motivated to be successful. By planning your day you can you can communicate this to your line manager in advance, and therefore remove some of the over management. Without some success in the role being demonstrated, the line manager will not change their style of management, ie they will not start to trust you enough to move their style from direction to perhaps delegation.

So what is *Plan Do Review*?

The concept is straightforward. You make a list of the tasks you have to complete and plan them in a S.M.A.R.T way. You let everyone one know what your plan is, communicating it to both your staff and your manager. The key to managing you manager is explained further in Chapter six. The next element of the *Plan Do Review* process is to actually work your plan, this is where the S.M.A.R.T element comes into its own, and the key to the plan is to make it achievable, and consider "what if".

Finally, you review your plan, this is the first element of the following days planning stage, by reviewing what you have, and more importantly, have not completed, and you will start the basis of your next plan.

The Plan Do Review model is a very good short term planning tool, ideal for day-to-day management, S.M.A.R.T works for both short term and long term or project management. For long term and Project management we discuss the value of a SWOT analysis later in the chapter

What is S.M.A.R.T?

S.M.A.R.T is an acronym for *Specific, Measurable, Achievable, Realistic and Time based.*

Specific; the task or job must be to the point. *Measurable*; there must be a success criteria. *Achievable;* There is no point planning something for which you will not complete, you are just setting yourself up for a fall. *Realistic;* you need to have a relevant and pertinent reason for doing the job in a certain way. It needs to be matter of fact. *Time based;* the task or plan needs to be delivered in a period allowed.

Before we go on to discuss long term planning I would like you to take some time to consider your own job, and think about a general day you have and the types of tasks you need to achieve in that day. Consider the Plan-do-review model and SMART tool, and reflect on how you would Plan your day using these skills. Perhaps you could consider a day you have had recently, perhaps one that didn't go as well as you would have liked… re plan it, see what you could have done differently…

Longer term planning

Short term planning is a very good tool for all managers, day-to-day stuff needs to be ordered in an A to Z way. However, short term planning is not enough; it is like a band releasing an album but each song being in an unrelated different style… Like ACDC doing a boy band ballad, then a duet with Michael Ball, it just doesn't work. What I am trying to say is that you need a theme to your work, or rather a vision.

The basis of long term planning for me, in my experience, is to first understand the problem or the task in hand. To determine the current picture of your professional situation, the best method to breakdown the issues comes in the shape of a S.W.O.T analysis.

What the hell is a S.W.O.T analysis I hear you say? It is a method of understanding the task you have, and breaking it down. By looking at the whole picture of the problem and breaking it down into Strengths, Weakness', opportunities and Threats. It takes the form of a set of four boxes on a page. Each containing one of the elements of the SWOT; one with strength, one weakness' etc. Moreover, you consider your task or job's attributes in each of the categories, for example, you may want to consider your staff as a strength, if they are established perhaps, or they maybe a weakness if they're all new to the role or perhaps you have a new company and no one really has any experience. Either way, you would list them in bullet point form in the relevant box...

Below is an example SWOT analysis

S	W
Staff experience Great line manager New Equipment	New Senior manager Wages split – poor Waste controls – poor Sales Plan – Tough Expenses Line – over spent
O	T
New Financial year – new budget Full compliment of staff	Competitor – new product launch Recession – little money in the economy.

With the S.W.O.T analysis on the previous page, there are a set of ground rules that need to be considered prior to the SWOT being created.

SWOT Rules

1. All SWOT analysis must produce an Action Plan
2. The S & W boxes must be concerned with internal positives & negatives
3. The O & T boxes must be concerned with external positives & negatives.

The key to dealing with a SWOT is that you need to have an action plan to counter the weakness', to capitalise on the opportunities and to guard against the threats.

The easy way to remember this is simple; you need to turn all of the W.O.T's into Strengths.

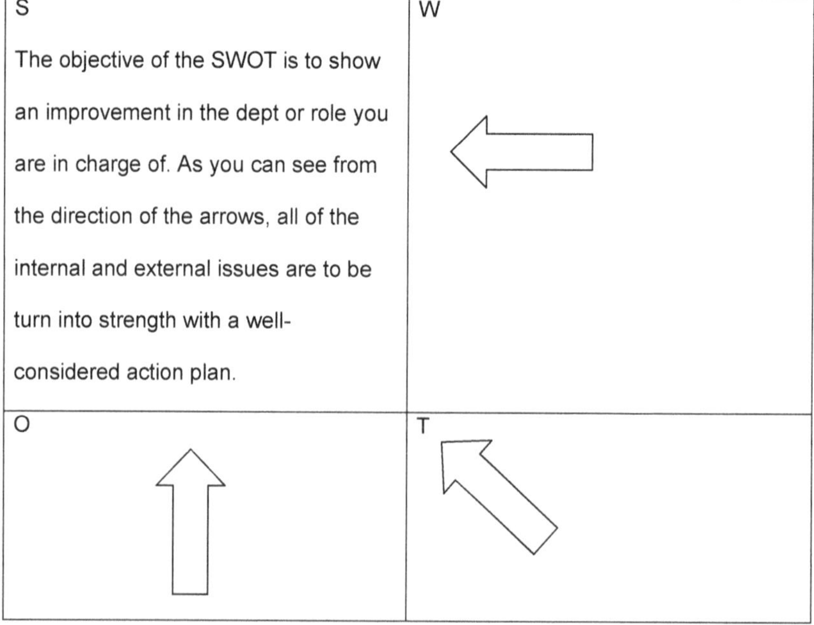

S	W
The objective of the SWOT is to show an improvement in the dept or role you are in charge of. As you can see from the direction of the arrows, all of the internal and external issues are to be turn into strength with a well-considered action plan.	
O	T

A couple of other thoughts for Swots' and action plans.

Consider the acronym PEST when building a SWOT. PEST is an acronym for *People, Environment, System,* and *Technology.* In an Ideal S.W.O.T., you would have at least two of each of the PEST elements in each of the SWOT Boxes. Therefore, two people strengths, two people weakness' etc it should give you at least 32 points on the swot. This is the ideal, however, in most cases you may not get this many points, but it does give you a great start.

Once you have the SWOT, and therefore the basis of your Action Plan, you then need to ensure that the actions to improve or correct the Weakness, opportunities' and Threats are all S.M.A.R.T.

Having considered *people* issues, *environmental* issues, *systems* or *technology* Strengths' and weakness', opportunities and threats, then determined your SWOT. Then from the said SWOT analysis formulate an action plan with at least one action or task per entry on the SWOT.

For your action plan, you need the following headings;

Task	Detail	Who	When	Measure.

Task; The Task is the bullet point from your SWOT.

Detail; the detail is how you are going to tackle the task.

Who; this is who is accountable for or completing the task.

When; this is the date the tasked is agreed to be completed by or the deadline.

Measure; this is the success factor, how it should look when it is complete.

Below is an example of the layout of your action plan,

Task	Detail	Who	When	Measure
Expense line	Reduce the expense overspend and hit budget	JD	Ongoing End wk52	The budget is to be on target. Stretch would be to be below target
Waste split	Current waste split is poor. Need to change the mindset of the team, and impact the year to date numbers	JD and team	Ongoing End Wk 52	Impact on the split and action and improve YTD. Stretch; below budget.

In the ideal, you would produce a plan based upon what you find and decide from your SWOT, then you would ideally have four-page plan based upon the PEST topics, so all of your environment corrections or actions would be on a single page.

One final thought on planning, is a more advanced type of planning is to create a vision for employees and subordinate manager to believe in. This can be very difficult for a new manager to do, so this is really for information only.
A vision is the kind of plan that a Leader makes, rather than a manager. Managers tend to be do-ers, people who make things happen, very much in the thick of things. Working a set resource to a set target. Leaders on the other hand, tend to be the setters of the targets, believing in what can be, rather than what needs to be. When creating a vision, you use the same steps as the manager would, SWOT, action plan. Etc. However, the key change in creating a vision for me is that you set out the end objectives, and allow the managers you have

under you to write their own plans to achieve these objectives. This is key to the while process of a vision and a leadership role. Without engaging your managers and allowing their natural motivation towards becoming better planning and achieving, then as a leader you will de motivate these manager and come no where near the vision you have set. I have seen over the years many leader managers make the massive mistake of trying to control every detail that happens, they tend finally to become over whelmed and actually achieve nothing. Without this trust and engagement of managers, you will also not grow your next generation of top managers. Affecting the long-term security of the company. Planning at the basic level is a great exercise for future managers, remember, that the longer the root on the plant, the better the plant does. This applies to experience in planning.

One final thought on planning and your life balance is the important/urgent model. This is a very simple way of prioritising what you do first. Below is the graphic that helps you understand the principle.

Urgent/important | Not urgent/important

Quadrant 1	Quadrant 2
Quadrant 3	Quadrant 4

Urgent/not important | Not urgent/not important

The graphic is in four parts, or quadrants, each quadrant represents demand or pressure of a particular task. For example if a task is overdue and a high priority then it would sit in quadrant 1. If you look at the quadrants, you will begin notice that each looks at urgency and importance in different states, ie either urgent or not urgent and then important or not important. And the four quadrants cover the combinations of these two states. If you look at this from a work point of view, than you will then begin to see that the 3rd and 4th quadrants are not important to your job role, so it may be concerning you home life. For example, you may need to pay a utility bill, and it is overdue, now from a work point of view this is urgent but not important. Talking to one of your colleagues about what you did on Saturday night, from a work point of view, is not important nor is it urgent. Both of these examples would sit in the 3rd and 4th quadrants from a work point of view! As previously mentioned, if a task is overdue and a high priority at work, then it would sit in quadrant 1. Similarly, if the same project were not overdue and high priority then it would sit in quadrant 2.

So how would you use this model? Simple you ask yourself which quadrant any task or demand upon you should sit. It is also worthy to note that you can apply quadrant process to your home life too, in both your working life and home life, then successful managers only operate in quadrant 2.

Chapter Four

The drowning man

The drowning man is a metaphor I used to describe motivation. Chapter four is, surprise, surprise about motivation, every person, every situation, every decision is driven by motivation.

So what is motivation? Motivation is a state of mind about a situation or an individual. As with any state of mind or train of thought, there are both positive and negative outcomes. Everyone is motivated on every thing, either positive (ie driven to complete a task) or negative (ie dragging behind on a project).

So, as a manager you need to firstly understand motivation as a concept, but also Identify others motivations and motivators. However, the most important single tool to managing motivation is to be able to create positive motivation in your self, your staff and your boss.

So how do you create motivation?

The simple answer is you don't. You can't create motivation, only influence it.

The chapter is call the drowning man, and I want to explain why I have titled a chapter on motivation with a negative experience. Consider the following;

You are a fully clothed non-swimmer, out of your depth. You are trying to keep yourself a float; you are expending a great deal of energy and time on the treading water element and not moving closer to the shore. There are people trying to help you, sending you various floatation devices. This will support you for a while. The problem with these “crutches” is that as the seascape never stays the same. A crutch that works in the calm may not be so sturdy in the swell. Then as the swell becomes rougher and rougher, the floatation aid fails... if you failed to support yourself in the calm, and only coped in chop with your donated armbands then in the rough you will drown.

So how does this example explain motivation? Motivation is about balance, and most young or new managers consider adding positives as a way of driving motivation. Whilst on the surface this is a good, if a little short sighted, way of improving motivation. Nevertheless, *the actual way to drive motivation is to remove the negatives.*

Below is a graphic, which may help you to understand the principle.

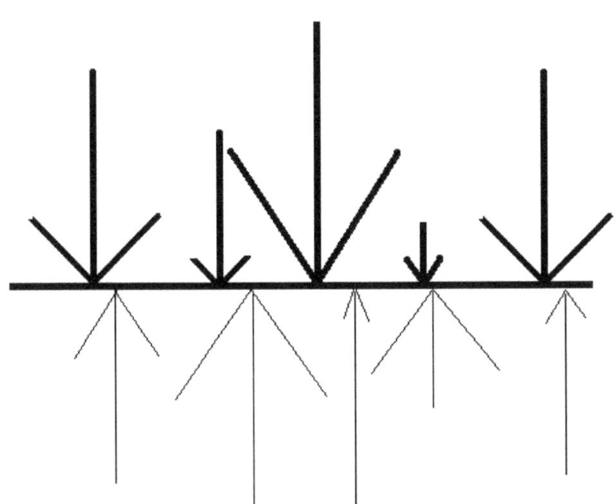

The line in the centre is the current motivation of the person our situation, and the arrows beneath are the positive motivators, and the arrows above are the negative motivators.

To influence motivation, as already discussed, the correct way to do this is to remove negative motivations or barriers, which are preventing the motivation level from rising.

If we go back to the drowning man example and consider removal of negatives, then the best approach any helper could have given the man was to help him remove his clothes and therefore enable him to be more efficient at treading water, or give him advice on treading water (training). As the example points out, if you try and support the drowning man with extra aids the eventually the aids fail or become over whelmed.

To put this into a real life situation, you the new manager, may have had a salary increase to support you in your new role. This will for a short time, give you a boost to your motivation. However, in the longer term when the job becomes harder (chop), it may keep you going, but as the job gets harder and harder (in the rough), you will still sink. So, instead of money, what will help you remove the barriers to you being self motivated? Well, I would like you to get a sheet of paper and a pen, and draw the line in the centre. Now, have a good think about the things that motivate you. Once you have a list of your motivators, apply each one an arrow, the size of the arrow is dependent upon how much it motivates you. I.e. the bigger the motivator, the bigger the arrow. Now on the other side, repeat the process with your negative motivations.

Usually, you will have more de motivators than motivators. Now you have your list, decide which of the de motivators are the easiest for you to remove. If for example, one of your de motivators is training, or lack of it, then go and learn about the subject you feel is holding you back. Once you have removed just one of your de-motivators, your natural motivators will help you float, or move your line up the page.

Earlier in the chapter, we talked about everyone and every situation being driven by motivation. Therefore, instead of listing your own motivations go back to your sheet of paper, turn it over and draw a new line. Think of a situation, for example an interview, where you need to influence someone else's motivation. By simply thinking about what motivates and de-motivates other people in a certain situation, then you can start to remove their de-motivators or in terms of an interview, doubts. This logic can be applied to your staff, your customers and your boss. By thinking about what each of them needs to help them "float", you will be removing there de-motivators. They will no longer be in danger of drowning, however rough it gets.

Chapter Five

The People

The biggest resource, expense and headache for any manager or business are its people - fact. The grass roots people have the greatest of impacts upon a company's fortunes of any of its employees. The best managers understand the needs of their people, by being understanding and considerate of the needs of the people you will drive the motivation of the people. As we have just reading the drowning man, by taking away the negative elements of the motivation you will naturally allow your people to be successful! In turn, successful people mean a successful business.

So how do you go about understanding the people?
People consider everything in terms of the positive and the negatives. It is either a good experience or a bad experience. The problem is that it is not a fifty-fifty split. Consider some research done about customer service; good service received by people will only be communicated to an average of three other people, where as bad customer service will be communicated to an average of twelve other people. – I guess no news really does mean good news.

As we can see from the research into customer service people tend to dwell on the negatives and a poor manager can very quickly damage the working ethic and motivation of the people by making some very basic mistakes.

Some of the key complaints from staff are as follows:-

1. Lack of planning
2. Work for works sake
3. My manager does not listen to me
4. I have not been trained
5. He or she expects too much.

I could start to list you a massive list of ways in which you can improve your relations with your staff. However, the only piece of advice I want to actually give you is ***to listen***. You have two ears and only one mouth, and as such, you should use them in that order. As discussed, in chapters three and four, we looked at planning and motivation, most staff need and want, to be directed in the work place. By having that plan, by listening to the people and understanding their needs and removing their de-motivators you will gain trust. Trust in their manager will increase the success and the emotional loyalty that is absolutely vital between a manager and their staff.

Whilst listening is key, there are times when you need to talk. A Buddha style Zen manager is fine, but if you say nothing then you are as bad, if not worse than a manager who says too much! The way you talk to staff, and more importantly question them, is critical to gaining the staff's emotional loyalty. I want to focus on the style of question that you ask, and the correct way to ask to get the best out of people.

So, how do you ask a question?

All managers should have a basic understanding about questions, ie how to use open and closed questions.

I want to focus on open questions mainly, but there is a place for closed questions, when you need a yes or no answer, when you don't need any information, just compliance of the member of staff.

Open questions are information seeking questions, all open questions start with the following five words;

What

Where

Why

When

Who

For a long time, it was considered that the best questions to ask were open questions, as the person being asked them, in comparison to closed questions, saw them as less aggressive. However, I would like to point out that of the five main open questions words, only one is truly not considered aggressive. The only question I would expect the successful manager to use is "What".

There is a great book I read called “the Power of what”, which the concept is fully explored. I am not going to dwell on this, but what I will say is that it works, “What” is a fantastic question to ask anyone. With some practice you can ask anything of anyone with the “what Question!”

So, considering what you have read so far in chapters 3, 4 and 5 I hope you are beginning to build a picture of some of the tips and tools that a new manager needs to be using. So far by planning, listening to your people and removing they things or barriers for them to be motivated, you will begin to succeed. Again, all of these tools and methods are inter linked, and compliment each other.

Chapter Six

Heading the Indians off at the Pass

The classic western film phrase is the inspiration for chapter six, when the hero rides out to meet the incoming enemy before they have a chance to spring the trap! This chapter is about managing you boss. Whilst I am not saying that they are the enemy nor are they trying to entrap you. However, what I am saying is that you should be taking the information to them before they ask for it or find out from someone else or themselves!

This is a simple concept, but is does have its origins in the planning of your day. Consider chapter 3, when we discussed planning, and in particular Plan – Do – Review. You as a line manager or subordinate manager will have a manager above you; they will outline your role or duties for you and expect you to plan your day accordingly, ensuring the correct and economic use of the resources that you command. Now, in the real world, you are likely to have failed or at least under performed or come across an unconsidered problem or difficulty. This is the nature of the Job of a manager, because if all of our days went well and uneventfully, there would be no need of a middle or subordinate manager.

It is these problems and difficulties I want to talk to you about, and the way you manage your boss' expectations.

Life has a way of throwing you the odd curve ball from time to time. As a manager when these hiccups happen they can leave the best laid plans in tatters, and reduce that hard-earned respect and trust you have been building up with your boss into shreds. You need to control the release of this information on these hiccups or plans to the boss. *Ie head the Indians off at the pass.*

When the plan you have in place does a mach2 nosedive in to the crapper, you need to jump to the review element of the Plan-Do-Review model, as your plan has not worked, for whatever reason, the fact that it has not worked is really a secondary issue at this stage. What the absolute critical issue is now is to ensure that you have learned by your mistake(s) or mishap(s) and doing something about it/them. This is a basic and necessary skill if you want to stay in the role you have, or indeed progress to the next level.
As with the plan do review cycle, the next element in this cycle, after review, is to plan. Therefore, when you next see you boss (and this is critical), with you bearing the bad news of the failure of the pervious plan (or the unexpected event that have thrown things out of shape), you need to not only tell them what has gone wrong, but more importantly, let them know what you are going to do about it.

So how do I let the boss know what the current situation is? Well firstly, you need to be checking. As managers, we are paid to check, by checking and re checking you will be able to understand the issues and be able to advise on any solutions. By staying close to the project you will know when the unexpected happens. When it does, you need to find out why and then have a short term and long-term solution.

The short-term solution is going to correct the problem or mistake, but if you do not adjust your long-term plan then the issue may arise again. Therefore, a permanent fix is also required. Consider for a moment that you wait for your boss to find out about the problem independently. Then they come to you to find out why? What do you think they will be thinking, or rather feeling, about you as the person they have entrusted this responsibility too. Remember that they too are a manager, and also paid to check, so by burying your head in the sand you will be setting yourself up for a rather large fall.

How do you think you would feel when he or she is asking you questions, or handing out you a solution? Well, you will feel pretty stupid, and more importantly, you'll have damaged your reputation and become less able or trustworthy in their eyes.

The key to managing the manager is to head them off at the pass, by going to them, keeping them informed, and in some instances, over informed. By making sure that you are and inviting them to see the successful outcome of a task or job, when it is at its finest. In the event that you are reporting bad news or a failure, you should go armed with the short-term action that you are taking, and in addition, the long-term plan for the issues you need to fix. This is a very “pro active” approach to being a manager and a skill that is core at the heart of every successful manager.

Chapter Seven

They Also Ran

This chapter is dedicated to anyone who has made a mistake, dropped a clanger, fumbled the ball, or generally made a cock up.

Mistakes, they are a fact -of -life. Everyone has made a mistake or two in their time. The key to mistakes is to consider them a learning experience. This was first explained to me when I attended a training session for the second company I every worked for. The trainer related the mistake as a learning process in the following story.

In the 1970's, a young computer programmer got a job at a new computer company in the United States. He was straight out of college and this was his first job. He was working on the operating system of the companies new control program for there latest model of computer when, whilst shutting down for the day, he accidently deleted the entire program from the computer tape.

The next morning, when the programmer arrived in the building at work. He was summoned to his Boss's office to answer for the mistake he had made. The programmer was expecting to be fired, and escorted off the premises.

When he arrived in the office of his boss, he was asked to sit down and the boss outlined to him that he had just cost the company over a million dollars in lost time and effort and could put the whole company out of business.

The programmer was very sorry for what had been a simple mistake. After the Boss had finished outlining his annoyance at the mistake made he instructed the programmer to get his behind back down to his office and get the program re written in record time. The programmer was amazed. He left the office apologising and assuring as he went. Later that day having written the computer program like a demon, the programmer wondered why he was still employed, and decided to go and see his boss to find out why.

So five minutes before the end of the day the programmer knocked on the door of his boss.

The boss opened the door and invited him in. The programmer started by telling his boss about his progress on the program since the morning and comparing it to the original program. At the end of this pitch, the programmer asked his boss why he was still employed. The boss looked at him and said, "Why would I fire you? I have just spent over a million dollars on your training!" The programmer never forgot what he had done; he went on to re create the award winning and landmark program, which in turn catapulted the company into the business stratosphere. 25 years on, the programmer became the chairperson of the company.

The moral of the story is that every one makes mistakes. How we respond to those mistakes as managers is critical. Think back to when you were a child, how did your mother teach you to walk? Did she chastise you every time you fell over? On the other hand, did she pick you up and dust you down, and show you and support you? If she had not helped you, or she had criticised you, then in all probability you would still be crawling around on all fours.

Failure in many instances is a great way to learn about something, if you look at learning experiences, either academic or skill based, each of the these methods of training allows people to make mistakes and learn from them, for example in exams or tests, projects etc. So, why as managers do we get frustrated and angry with staff that make mistakes? The example in story of the programmer, for me highlights two key issues; the employee will be very well motivated after you have been lenient with them. They will generally want to repay your kindness and the potential of any positive employee is limitless.

Secondly, they will generally have learned something from the experience, so failure = learning!

Have you ever been back to a former place of employment and caught up with former colleagues? Moreover, have you ever been amazed at the change or the progress of those people since your last visit? On the other hand, have you ever reflected upon your own progress through life either at work or in education? The “also ran's” in horseracing, continue to run after you have moved on, and eventually they become the winners. When considering mistakes in the work place, you the new manager, would be wise to be calm, and use the “what” question techniques to ask the employee who has made the mistake what their plan is to put it right? It will motivate the employee, act as a positive learning experience and generally be good for the business. This is a no brainer for me.

Chapter Eight

The Success – o – meter

So, In the boss' office there is a game show style gauge that shows every manager how great they are doing. In addition, every time they do a fantastic job, a light goes off and all the bells and whistles chime! Yeah Right! If only that was the case!!!

The fact of the matter is that every manager needs a gauge to measure their success. Every company I have ever worked for has a standard method for each of their managers to be measured. The simple point I am going to make is that, you need to make sure that you start with the end in mind, What I mean by this is that to be able to succeed you need to ensure that you are working towards the goals that are set for you and be able to prove that you have moved in that direction. Steven Covey Covers this subject in his excellent book, the seven step of highly effective people. It is well worth buying a copy!

When I have explained this to my trainees in the past, I have likened it to taking a journey;

Consider the following three drivers Tom, Dick and Harry. Tom, he gets up and packs up the car and jumps on in the drivers seat and starts the car. He drives off, usually as fast as he can. The harder he drives the car the quicker he will get there, or so he thinks.

Dick, he gets up and packs up the car and jumps on in the drivers seat and starts the car. He drives off, usually as fast as he can. Half way through the day, Dick stops the car at the services, he reaches for the map in the glove box. He looks around and finds out where he is, then where he needs to be. However, looking at the map he has a chance of getting to his destination. Harry, now Harry gets up, makes himself a cup of tea, and considers his journey. He reaches for the map, plans his route to his destination. When he has finished, he packs the car and jumps on in the driving seat. By understanding where he needs to be he can make the best use of his journey, both in terms of time and expense.

I would ask my trainees at that this stage who they think will get to the destination first. It really is a no brainer as it will be Harry. Then I ask them how they think the story applies to them and their performance reviews. They all claim to be Harry!

Earlier in the book, I discussed Planning. If we consider Tom, Dick and Harry as types of manager, then Tom is the kind manager who works very hard, but without any direction or plan. This type of manager will not ever get to their destination. They will not make the grade when it comes to proving their work output at review time. Now Dick's example, Dick is very similar to Tom, he too is a very hard worker, however, Dick realises that he has a review coming up and takes the opportunity to review his current performance. In the example, Dick may well have taken the wrong direction in the first instance, and as such, he still has a full journey to take. Consider this in the work place, if Dick changes his direction say half way through the business quarter, then he may have to put some long hours in to reach the results he requires. Even so, time has passed, and results whilst in the green at the end of the quarter, they could have been consistent and green from the start. In addition, any extra effort or resources used may increase or incur extra costs. Just like Dick would have done in fuel! Harry, he is the SMART manager, he has planned his route, he first understood what his objectives were, and planned accordingly. Of our three drivers, he would have reached his target in the shortest time, and with the least amount of cost spent.

To summarise, if you want the success – o – meter to be singing your praises in the boss' office, well you will need to plan your route before you start!

Planning in the short term for you is easy. All managers are not lone drivers, they are bus drivers, and being able to organise all of the passengers to the right stops takes a route or a vision, which brings us to the next chapter.

Chapter Nine

Lighting the fire and fanning the flames

So how do you as a manager become a leader manager? What is a Leader manager? If you consider the name, Leader Manager, it is made up of two names, Leader and Manager. A leader by definition is a person that leads others; a manager is someone that manages a process.

Therefore, a leader manager is someone that leads others in completing a task or project. So how do you become this leader manager? Well, for starters you need to have an objective or destination that you want your people or project to reach. You will need to be able communicate this vision and motivate the people to complete the required steps to get to the objective.

Think back to Tom Dick and Harry, each of their objectives were clear, yet only Harry achieved his destination in the time allowed.

Think about some of the great leaders in history, none of them actually physically did anything fantastic; however, they had a vision of what they wanted to create and when they needed to create it. Wartime leaders do not actually shoot the enemy; however, they inspire and encourage the troops to do it! Another great example of a leader is a football manager, he is on the bench, he has no input into the game once the teams walk on to the pitch, so his team talk or tactical vision has to inspire his players to do there best on the pitch. Even before the whistle is blown by the referee the players captain is making a decision about which team goes into bat or which team kicks off first. The players need to know what the manager is thinking about each decision made through out the match, without communication face to face. This is Vision.

So how do you relay this vision? In my experience you need to start with the destination, then and this is important, ask your team what they can do to drive this. Remember we talked about listening? As a leader manager you need to listen to you team, whilst some of the idea's may not be in the theme of your vision, the team will be motivated by the vision if some of their idea's are included. Also by being motivated, they will want to deliver the whole vision for you.

So you have told the team what you want to achieve, they have helped you plan the route to achieve the vision. So how do you gauge the progress? The key to gauging the progress is to break every task down into what the task is, who is doing it, when it needs to be done, and what the measure of success is. We have discussed this earlier in the book, it is important that this plan is agreed with the team, and it is built from a SMART point of view. The final part of being that leader manager is to allow your team to deliver; it is a very poor manager that uses their team member's failures to keep them in trim. It is usually a sign that the leader manager has not listened.

Chapter Ten

Trick Shots

So how do you put all of the lessons together? That is what this chapter is about. You can use, and should use, most of the tricks in your day-to-day working life, however, I am going to list some instances where you can tie the tools together and get the upper hand.

The first day on the job

On the first day of the job, you will not know what to expect. You will be meeting new people, finding out the lie of the land, and lets face facts you are being judged by both staff and management. So you need to make a good impression. The first day is your chance to set out your stall, with this in mind, you need to start the day by using the "managing you" concepts from chapter 3. So understand what you want people to think of you. Also from chapter three, on your first day you need to be looking at how the department or team currently functions, to do this you need to be using the concepts of the "drowning man" and "the people" chapters, Listen first, ask the right questions in the right way and understand the motivations of just about everyone. This is a big ask, and you will as the days and weeks go by get more information, but you will be surprised by how much you will get over time. The last thing you want to do is say or demand too much at this stage, ease your self into the role, remember Tom, he sets off without a plan and ends up lost.

The job role defined

You will have been landed into the role, and your perceptions are set and you arrive at your first meeting with your new boss. Firstly, you need to consider their motivation, if you don't understand you boss then you will never meet and then surpass their expectations. Consider chapter 4, "the drowning man" and Chapter 6, "heading the Indians off at the pass". You need to work with your boss, they have your future in their hands.

Managing managers

You maybe put into a role that evolves you managing a team of managers, The key to managing managers rather than staff, is that each of these people is driven, and has a need or hunger to succeed. If you do not have a vision, or you over manager the managers then they will become less productive and in many instances stale. If you use "lighting the fire and fanning the flames" , become the football manager instead of the captain, then each of your "players" will pull in the direction you have envisaged, remembering that they too have a team to manage and need also to motivate their players too.

The big Picture/being Harry

Once you have gotten over your first few days or weeks, then you will need to start progressing, you will need to have a plan. Therefore, you will need to combine "managing you", "The people", "the drowning man" and the "lighting the fire" chapters, plan, do it and review it. Whilst motivating your people and communicating the big picture. You need to have invested your first few weeks in understanding the dynamic of your role and your team. By using this time to learn you will be being Harry!

When things don't go right.

We have talked about failure in the book, and you will fail. This is a natural process, and the fact that you do not have it right is not the actual failure, the failure is not to do anything about the situation. When things do not go as planned, use "managing you" and a huge dollop of "heading the Indians off at the pass". Think about "the drowning man", take out the biggest de motivator(s) to the situation, yours, your staffs and your boss's. Finally remember, "They also ran"

There are literally hundreds of situations that you can use the tools and tricks that I have disclosed in the book. In addition, there are so many more methods out there. However, it is not the mandate of the book to discuss all of them, and besides there is no fun with out a little trial and error in finding what works. You have enough to start you on your journey to becoming a successful manager, and I would love to hear from any of you that use the book and your experiences of it. So much so that anyone who would like to send me his or her comments or stories please do so by e-mail to jason@pilotbank.co.uk, I can't guarantee a reply but I will read them all, and maybe include them in any future editions of the book.

Good luck and happy managing!

Jase

www.ingramcontent.com/pod-product-compliance
Ingram Content Group UK Ltd.
Pitfield, Milton Keynes, MK11 3LW, UK
UKHW041837200726
13854UKWH00003BA/1178

9 781445 219226